FAMOUS *Animals*

BRAVE, LOYAL, KIND

Since early times, people and animals have
often had very special relationships.
Throughout history there have been many true
stories about the bravery, loyalty, kindness,
and intelligence of animals. Here are just a
handful of such stories. There are many
other animals whose tales have not
been told, but whose deeds
have been just
as great.

3

BARRY THE BRAVE

The woman and child lay deep
in snow, completely buried by
the avalanche. They couldn't
survive much longer in the
chilling cold. Suddenly, the
woman felt a warm tongue
brushing her frostbitten
face. As she looked up,
she saw the massive
head of a dog.

The woman took
her little boy, wrapped
him in a shawl, and
tied him to the dog's back.
The dog pushed through
the snow with his precious
cargo, finally delivering the
little boy to safety.

Barry, a Saint Bernard, was the most famous mountain-rescue dog ever. He was born in 1800 and, during his lifetime, rescued more than forty people in the mountains of Switzerland.

Barry was trained at a **monastery** in the Swiss Alps. The monks taught their guard dogs to search for travelers lost in the snow. Saint Bernards still carry out this brave work today.

GREYFRIAR'S BOBBY

The wind howled like a mad
wolf around the deserted
graveyard. The small shaggy
dog tucked his head between
his paws and gave an
involuntary shiver,
but he didn't budge
from his master's
grave. Not until
the boom of the
one o'clock gun
sounded did he dash
across the road to
grab some bread from
an innkeeper. He then
returned immediately
to keep a lonely
vigil by his master's
resting place.

Bobby was a little Skye terrier who belonged to John Gray, an Edinburgh policeman. In 1858, John Gray died, and was buried in the Greyfriar's churchyard in Edinburgh. For fourteen years, Bobby watched over his master's grave, leaving only at lunchtime or if the weather was bad. When Bobby died in 1872, he was buried near his master in the churchyard. Today, a statue stands in nearby Candlemaker Row, in memory of his loyalty.

JUMBO THE ELEPHANT

The children sat with their eyes glued to the ring. The Greatest Show on Earth had just begun beneath the circus big top. They had seen clowns, trapeze artists, dancing horses, jugglers, and lion tamers, but the star of the show was still to appear. Then a great cheer went up. There he was – the largest animal they had ever seen – Jumbo the elephant! Slowly, the massive elephant walked around the ring, stretching out his long trunk to gently touch the children as he passed.

Jumbo, an African elephant, lived more than one hundred years ago – from 1861 to 1885. He is believed to be the largest land animal ever kept in captivity. He measured ten feet tall at the shoulder.

Jumbo spent most of his life at the Regent's Park Zoo in London, where he was a favorite with children. Despite his enormous size, he was very kind and gentle, and he loved children. He took them for rides on his back in a special seat called a howdah.

In 1882, the zoo sold Jumbo to showman P.T. Barnum, who took the elephant back to America to perform in his famous traveling circus. Thousands of people turned up to say good-bye, showering Jumbo with gifts of his favorite foods – candy and sweet rolls. In America, Jumbo soon became the greatest star of the Greatest Show on Earth.

Today, Jumbo's name remains part of the English language and means anything that is very big, such as a jumbo jet or a jumbo pizza.

11

THE GALLIPOLI DONKEY

Gunfire rang out along the slopes of Shrapnel Gully. Soldiers huddled in their trenches, waiting for the gunfire to cease. Wounded soldiers lay in **no-man's-land** *in the direct line of gunfire. Through the noise and dust, a man appeared, followed by a little donkey with a Red Cross band tied around its ears. Fearlessly, the pair made their way across the battlefield. A wounded man was gently lifted onto the donkey's back, and carried to safety through a hail of bullets and thudding mortars!*

More than 200,000 soldiers from the **Allies** lost their lives in the tragic Gallipoli Campaign of World War I. But many were saved by an Australian soldier named Simpson and his little donkey. Time and time again, the pair defied death to rescue the wounded from the front lines. Today, a statue of a man with a donkey stands in Canberra, Australia, in memory of their courage, bravery, and determination.

ROB THE PARA-DOG

The black-and-white dog waited eagerly at his handler's side as the plane droned on through the night. Finally, the dispatch door of the plane opened and soldiers began to adjust their parachutes and prepare for the drop. The soldier in front of the dog leaped into the night. With a word from his handler, the dog launched himself out of the plane and into space. The wind whistled through his fur and pinned his ears flat against his head as he fell toward the ground. Abruptly, the parachute opened, jerking him up, then guiding him lightly to the ground.

Rob, or the Para-Dog, as he came to be known, made more than twenty parachute jumps into enemy territory during World War II. He served with the British Special Air Service, and jumped into North Africa and Italy. Once he had landed, Rob would lie perfectly still and quiet until his handler arrived and released him from his harness. Then he would find the rest of the patrol in the darkness and guard them on their dangerous missions. During one such mission in Italy, Rob led a whole group of soldiers to safety after it was feared they had been lost in battle.

Rob received the Dickin Medal for bravery, the Red Collar of the Royal Society for the Prevention of Cruelty to Animals, and six war ribbons, making him the only animal in British history to receive so many awards.

GI JOE THE PIGEON

The Allied pilots
prepared their bombers
for takeoff. The planes roared
into life, and the smell of airplane
fuel filled the air. As the pilots
waited for the final takeoff signal,
an exhausted little pigeon
flew into base. His feathers were
singed, and his heart beat like a
drum in his tiny chest. The bird carried
a vital message strapped to one leg:
Do not send the bombers. The area is
now in the hands of Allied soldiers!

GI Joe, America's most famous pigeon, was a hero. If the brave bird had been just a few minutes late, many soldiers would have been bombed by their own planes.

GI Joe was one of many homing pigeons that served in World War II. Homing pigeons played a major role as messengers and were responsible for saving many lives. Homing pigeons were also used on bombers. If a bomber was shot down, the pigeon would be released to fly back to base with a message showing the exact position of the plane so that the crew could be rescued.

After the war, GI Joe was
flown from America
to England and taken to
the Tower of London. There
he was presented with the
Dickin Medal for bravery.

OPO THE DOLPHIN

A crowd of children waded in the shallow waters. Their squeals of excitement could be heard up and down the beach as the dolphin quietly zigzagged between them. Then, suddenly, she was off, racing out to deeper waters, where, much to the delight of the children, she hurled herself up into the air to perform a double somersault.

Opo the friendly dolphin turned up at the seaside settlement of Opononi, New Zealand, in the summer of 1955. Slowly, of her own accord, Opo began seeking out people to play with. Word of the dolphin quickly spread.

Soon, hundreds of people came to watch Opo play. She would juggle a brightly colored beach ball on her nose or flip empty bottles into the air. Opo was always kind and gentle with children and would allow them to pet her.

When Opo died, she was given a grand funeral. A statue to her memory was built on the shores of the local harbor.

Speaking with Koko

The huge, black gorilla gently cradled the tiny kitten to her chest. The kitten snuggled into the gorilla's fur and purred.

"Tell me about your pet," the research assistant asked the gorilla, using sign language.

"Soft," the gorilla signed back to the assistant.

"What kind of animal is it?" asked the assistant.

"Cat, cat, cat," the gorilla answered. "Soft, good cat, cat."

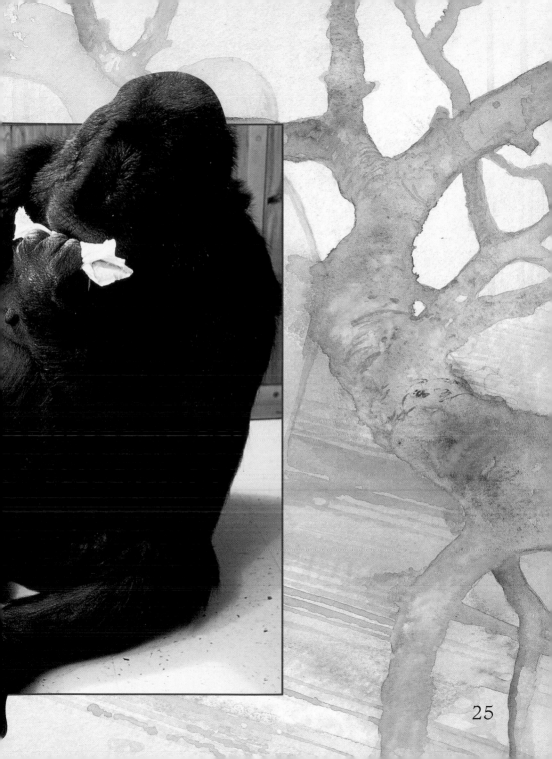

Koko the gorilla learned to speak using American Sign Language, which she was taught by her trainer and adopted mom, Dr. Penny (Francine) Patterson. Penny adopted Koko from the San Francisco Zoo in 1972, after Koko's own mother couldn't care for her.

When Koko was less than a year old, she was signing her first words: *food, drink,* and *more.* Eventually, Koko learned over five hundred signs, which she used to ask for things and to play jokes. Scientists were able to learn valuable information from Koko's behavior.

OLD BLUE

The small, coal black bird flitted down from her nest and landed on the man's shoulder, chirping away. He gave her a worm, which she took back to her nest, where three little beaks opened wide in unison to receive it. She plopped the worm into the nearest mouth and was off again to find more food for her brood.

Old Blue was a black robin. And by 1979, she was one of only five black robins remaining in the world.

During the 1980s, Dr. Don Merton and the New Zealand Wildlife Service set out to save the black robin. The last five birds were taken to an island so they could lay their eggs in safety. But only one bird – Old Blue – hatched any chicks. Old Blue was nine years old, although robins usually live only to be four or five.

With the help of the New Zealand Wildlife Service, Old Blue laid more eggs and mothered more chicks than any other black robin.

Today, there are more than two hundred black robins living on the Chatham Islands, and all of them are descendants of Old Blue.

Glossary

Allies – troops from countries that fought against Germany and its supporters in World Wars I and II

monastery – the place where monks work and live

no-man's-land – a stretch of land that lies between enemy lines during a war

vigil – guarding or keeping a watch over something

Index

FROM THE AUTHOR

I have always loved animals. So I had a lot of fun writing this book. The idea for the book came from a medal I inherited from my grandfather. He fought in the Gallipoli Campaign during World War I, and the medal was in honor of his bravery. On the medal is a donkey carrying a wounded man. I had always wondered about this little donkey, and wanted to find out more. My research introduced me to many true stories of animal courage and loyalty, inspiring me to write this book.

Susan Brocker

Imagine That!

Written by **Susan Brocker**
Illustrated by **Bryan Pollard** and **Genevieve Wallace** (pp. 14-15)
Photography by **Department of Conservation:** (pp. 28-29);
The Gorilla Foundation: (pp. 24-27); **Eric Lee-Johnson.:** (pp. 22-23);
PDSA: (pp. 20-21); **Photobank Image Library:** (pp. 3-5; p. 13; p. 17);
Robert Harding Picture Library: (p. 6); **Stock Photos Ltd.:** Jose Fuste
Raga (p. 2); **The Zoological Society of London:** (pp. 8-9; p. 11)

05 04 03 02 01 00 99
10 9 8 7 6 5 4 3 2 1

Published in the United States by

Rigby
a division of Reed Elsevier Inc.
500 Coventry Lane
Crystal Lake, IL 60014

Printed in Hong Kong
ISBN: 0-7901-1871-8